Poetry: It's a 'Shore' Thing!
In an Unsure World

An Anthology
of Micro-Memoirs
from the South Shore Poets
of Long Island

Co-Edited by
Paula Curci and Peter V. Dugan
with Foreword by
Dr. Pearl Ketover Prilik

ISBN: 978-0-9654831-6-2

Words With Wings Press
Long Island, New York

Front Cover Photo- Lisa Kandell
Back Cover Photo- Jim Coulter

This project was made possible by funds
from the Acoustic Poets Network™
Poet Laureate Visitation Project

Thank you to those who supported this project.

Poetry: It's a 'Shore' Thing!
In an Unsure World

The 'Shore' Story Micro-Memoir Project
is an anthology of micro-memoir poems and stories
from a community of poets who live
primarily in Long Beach, and nearby on the
south shore of Long Island, in Nassau County NY.

Shore Poets Open Mic Staff and Hosts
Paula Curci
Peter V. Dugan
Theresa Rosario-Berzner
Pearl Ketover Prilik
Doreen Dd. Spungin

Community Outreach
Harold Michelman
Carole Michelman
Nina Goldenberg
Pat Brown
Francine Rosen
Wayne Marcus
Pearl Ketover Prilik
Ralph Hooten
Jim Coulter
Nina Malkin

Special Thanks
To all our spouses
Jen Gibaldi
Nina Malkin
Jeannie Dillion
Mark Siegal

Submissions
Poetry: It's a *'Shore'* Thing!™
Poet Laureate Invitational Unplugged Open Mic

Shore Poets
Long Beach Public Library, Long Beach, NY
2nd Wednesday of each month
October 2023-July 2023

Special Shore Poet Events
Winter Solstice December 21, 2022
Nursing Home Outreach March 21, 2023
NCPLS Youth Award Ceremony June 14, 2023
Summer Solstice June 21, 2023
Ekphrastic Night with West End Arts July 12, 2023
With Kathleen Regan, Scott Ferrone, & Stu Friedman

Special Submissions:
April 2023 National Poetry Month

The Freeport Library Memoir Writers Group
Facilitated by Barbara Spinelli
Freeport Memorial Library, NY
April 11, 2023

The Performance Poets Association
Tuesdays with Poetry
Poetry as Memoir™ presentation by Paula Curci
Hosted by
Lorraine LoFrese Conlin and Doreen Dd. Spungin
Bellmore Memorial Library, NY
April 25, 2023

A Note From The Long Beach Public Library

The Shore Poets offer us a beautiful and compelling glimpse into memories—cherished and rare—that make us each uniquely human. It is in sharing that we touch one another's lives and this special volume speaks to the heart, not just the mind, of the reader. Bravo and brava to the poets whose voices bring these stories to life for us all to share, and who inspire us to do the same.

Sarah Siegel
Head of Programs and Marketing,
Long Beach Public Library

~

The Shore Poets Wish To Thank:

The Long Beach Public Library
Tara Lannen-Stanton
Jakea Williamson
Sarah Siegel
Nicole Menzzasalma
Natasha Drax
Madison Gusler
Louis Rodriquez
And the rest of the staff

Introduction
By Paula Curci

When I was affirmed the Poet Laureate of Nassau County for 2022-2024, I received a phone call from Peter V. Dugan, Nassau County Poet Laureate (2017-2019). He asked, "So, when are you starting your open mic?" Before we knew it, a wonderful group of poets helped shape the foundation of the Poet Laureate Invitational: "It's a 'Shore' Thing!"™ Open Mic. With their help and the support of Theresa Rosario-Berzner and Pearl Ketover Prilik, our first open mic successfully started on October 12th, 2022, at the Long Beach Public Library in Long Beach, NY.

It was a beautiful testament of resilience. We were all taking small steps toward reentering our post-pandemic life. At that time, people were still apprehensive about direct gatherings and attending live community programs. Amazingly, thirty people who had never met before joined together to share their voices.

In order to encourage participation, Peter and I brainstormed on how our program could be different from other open mics. We came up with the idea of having a fusion mic where people could write and listen at the same session. Poets were also invited to get loud with maracas, tambourines and other noisemakers that we provided.

Each month at our open mic, we asked participants to write a mini micro-memoir. A micro-memoir is a brief snapshot of a recollection, using a single story from one's life, written in the first person. We requested this poem or short narrative be in response to a prompt, and be composed on a 5 x 8 index card— hence: micro! It was decided that submission of one's 5 x 8 card at the end of the night was permission to publish, and we accepted all the "in the moment" responses we received.

The poetic writing prompts turned out to be much more than a fun, unusual activity. Our open mic drew poets, prose writers, singer songwriters, artists and improv actors as well. This eclectic mix of artists produced submissions of organic and raw memories. They transformed their recollections from a mental painting, recreating them as a story or poem. Moreover, most were miraculously written on the spot! When you realize that these petite stories represent the writers' first retrieved and tangible echo of a memory, you can understand how magical they are.

Memory retrieval is a neurological activity. So, understandably, some of our Shore Poets needed more time. Not everyone can marinate their memory on the spot and quickly retrieve the details they wish to write about. For those contributors, we agreed to extend the submission time. As long as they were in attendance when the prompt was given, they could deliver their micro-memoir at our next session. Like clockwork, those submissions came in at our very next meeting.

If memory is the writers' only resource, whether it be a six-line bio, an "I am" portrait poem, an autobiography—or in this case, a micro-memoir—it is rich with innate feeling and perception. Even if our memory needs time to materialize or is a bit skewed by the mind's propensity to embellish or minimize, it still holds great value. The poems and stories in this anthology confirm that fact!

The micro-memoir concept organically found its mission and manifested itself into a sociological perspective project. The open mic and the micro-memoir project's mission was to create community, with words, through acceptance and faith. Everyone who submitted trusted that their memory would be honored and respected.

What we found was that these writers were eager to participate; they wanted to dig deep for a memory to share. Moreover, by and large they chose to write about positive memories; their thoughts were wholesome, refreshing and uplifting. They shared about family and friends, so many good moments. They shared snippets of childhood and adult life that they may have never shared before.

After living in such an unsure world since 2020, this safe and accepting program was something we all needed. It is revered by all. This anthology is an example of how our South Shore poets, who have lived through such unsure times, from Hurricane Sandy to now, all have a belief that sharing their stories is cleansing and healing. Hence: "Poetry: It's a 'Shore' Thing!"*TM*

In this newfangled post-Covid environment, a phenomenon has occurred. Now more than ever, poets are activating their right to free speech and, in this case, demanding it be in a safe and peaceful place. I have found that people come to the podium to tell a story that lay dormant in their hearts for years. They come to speak, through their poems, prose or lyrics, to advocate for a cause, to own an emotion, to affirm a new journey or to be rid of a past fear. And in turn, they help, encourage and inspire others with their words.

Although we have been expressing ourselves at open mics for years, Peter V. Dugan and I have defined this movement as *Contemporary Expressionism*. And herein we have compiled a slice of American folk-life, to validate those dormant stories, those expressions. These are the stories that our micro-memoir project and our open mic environment have brought to life. Moreover, this anthology represents a microcosm of memories from poets who primarily live on the south shore of Nassau County, NY. How uniquely special it is to celebrate locally!

I am so proud of all of the writers who participated in this program; proud that we had the opportunity to chronicle their lives lived. I want to thank all those who contributed to *Poetry: It's a 'Shore' Thing: In an Unsure World*. Thank you for allowing us to see, through your lens, a personal account of your life. I hope you enjoy this mini, micro memoir. It is truly a "shore" story time capsule!

Paula Curci MS. Ed.
Nassau County Poet Laureate 2022-2024

FOREWORD:
by
Dr. Pearl Ketover Prilik

"....there are some things we can never assign to oblivion,
memories we can never rub away.
They remain with us forever, like a touchstone."
— Haruki Murakami - *Kafka on the Shore*

Memories are a touchstone from which we regain our sense of stability and familiarity. They also help us process trauma and metamorphize ourselves into a new present and face the future. *Poetry: It's a 'Shore' Thing! In an Unsure World* is a collection of such touchstones.

How ironic and fitting that the quote above is from a book with the word shore in its very title. *Kafka on the Shore* is a story about metamorphosis. What does all this have to do with a micro-memoir anthology? I believe that the personal and collective experience of the micro-memoir project was transformative, resulting in the volume you now hold in your hands.

As a psychoanalyst, poet and writer, and significantly as a participant-observer, I realized that this micro-memoir anthology had a deeper socio-psychological impact. After a long period of isolation, the "It's a *'Shore'* Thing!" gatherings and the micro-memoir writing project were a source of healing from the trauma of the Covid pandemic.

In the early days of re-emergence from Covid, folks yearned for a semblance of normalcy and predictability; the world was an unsure place in which to live. Many were unsure about health, the state of our lives going forward and of our connections to one another. For many it brought a sense of broken community and a questioning sense of self and identity in shaky times.

As Covid concerns receded, the question of re-emergence arose, bringing along even more uncertainty—with few of us unsure about what that correct and safe protocol was in this new world. How, indeed, could one be sure about when and if it was safe or simply worth it to venture out. I even asked myself whether it was worth the risk to attend a public gathering. Yet, in October 2022, a diverse group of people gathered for a monthly open mic.

Simply put, joy and connection and a sense of predictable normalcy rejoined the world. Readings were punctuated with supplied noisemakers, tambourines and supportive applause, and as feelings of warmth washed over the monthly assemblies like a welcome tide, a community began to form from a few intrepid souls.

If there remained uncertainty, one thing was sure: that a group of people would arrive each month ready to share and to listen, and that an innocuous pile of white index cards would open the doors of memory and provide an opportunity to document our collective lives and be permanently archived as our living shared memory

I experienced this activity of memoir writing, in a safe space, and its inspired rich sense of connectedness. Was it worth it? There was no doubt — it "shore" was! Micro-memoir writing is a complicated neurological activity shown to not only illustrate how events are processed, but how experience is shaped and impacted by our memory. This compilation reaches beyond neurologic sparking, forming a specimen of folklore that serves to define this group of spoken word artists that are now known as the Shore Poets.

The writing of memoirs has been found to organize thoughts and to stabilize mood. In the aftermath of the pandemic, I would suggest it re-established our sense of normalcy, identity and security. The micro-memoir activity organically became a welcome release from Covid, a way to reach back, remember and record important times and, for many of us, renew the collective good times of life on the South Shore.

A note on healing here is warranted: The human imperative to "heal the world" is echoed in many belief systems. It seems to me that one of the most positive aspects of the human spirit is this felt need to repair, heal and improve. Artists in particular have the ability to give voice and action to this drive. Therefore, I do not find it too grand a leap to see *Poetry: It's a 'Shore' Thing! In an Unsure World* as a creation of repair; born from the need to gather, to read, to listen, to write and to be together after isolation.

This anthology is a folklore document, a living testament, and tribute to a community that organically bloomed from the seeds of artists of all forms who obviously yearned to be heard. What began as a simple entertaining exercise at an open mic morphed into folklore, in that all poets and writers were collectively doing the same thing—writing about their lived lives together, and helped regain a sense of balance and certainty. If the world was still a bit unsure and uncertain, one's personal memories were absolutely a touchstone of familiarity and a revival of a sense of identity that might have been shaken, perhaps even shattered, during the pandemic.

I want to express enormous gratitude to Poet Laureate Paula Curci who, with the able assistance of Peter V. Dugan and Theresa Rosario-Berzner, made the Shore Poets a reality and this anthology possible, and in so doing manifested the understanding that truly .*"...there are some things we can never assign to oblivion, memories we can never rub away. They remain with us forever, like a touchstone."*— Haruki Murakami - *Kafka on the Shore*

It's a 'Shore' Thing
The 'Shore' Story project

OCTOBER 12, 2022

BEACH

Beach, Another Word for Yesterday

How sweet, despite the ocean's salt

How cool, despite the burning sun

Those summers greeted me,

a child so innocent.

They bid goodbye and I, no longer young,

move back to winters that try their best

to wrest from me the memories

that, to this day,

warm an aging heart.

Doreen Dd. Spungin
No. Woodmere, NY
Poet

The Vortex: National Boulevard Boardwalk, Long Beach, NY

Every summer, my niece came to visit us at the beach. We wanted her to experience riding bikes on the boardwalk, so we ventured out. As we passed the lifeguard station on National Boulevard, an unexpected storm started up.

The sand, next to the station, swirled in a tornado-like circular fashion and zipped up from the beach onto the planks of the boardwalk and around our bikes. It was like a monsoon! The coarse sand flew up in our faces, preventing us from seeing. We had to walk the bikes and we were drenched when we got home.

When Sandy hit, years later, that area was severely damaged. The lifeguard station was destroyed, and Governor Cuomo came to visit that street. To this day, my family calls that section of National Boulevard "the vortex."

Paula Curci
Long Beach, NY
Performance Poet
Nassau County Poet Laureate 2022-2024

Morning Toast, Long Beach, NY

Tips of ocean crests touch my toes
Breaking ground
for a new day
Champagne bubbles
at my feet
Dip by Dip
Sip by Sip
I drink it all in …
to the bottom of my sole

Nina Goldenberg
Long Beach, NY
Poet and Educator

Celebration of Summer's end
Somersaulting down beach dunes
Knowing I'll be back again

Sudden crisp September air
brings hurricane season,
returning to the city
and to school soon

Patricia Brown
Five Towns, NY
Poet

My Shore Story
September 10, 2001, Long Beach, NY, Boardwalk

Our usual, daily, post-dinner walk on Long Beach boardwalk
Suddenly weather morphing toward beastly, ominous
Sky turning dark, clouds moving frenetically
Rapid lightning strikes resembling violent scratches on a mirror
As squalls buffet us.

Me a lover of Mother Nature's wild side
But the elements that day were more vengeful than wild
Next day, my husband's birthday.
My belief about grim reaper and birthdays
Force me to return home

Nine-eleven, the calm after the storm
Spectacular sun-drenched morning
By nine a.m., lower Manhattan in ruins
Mayhem and chaos
Death and desperation

Had plans that night to celebrate
My husband's birthday
Was the nine-ten violent weather a portent to
The unprecedented nine-eleven tragedy?
I went on with my life.

Dr. Rohini B. Ramanathan
Oceanside, NY
Poet and Singer

5

Memory on the Beach

Wiggling my toes in the sand,
I spread out my blanket,
smooth it out with my hands.
Watching the waves come onto the shore,
hearing the swoosh as they return to the sea.
Feeling the warmth of the sun, heating my skin.
The drops of perspiration run,
down the length of my neck and chin,
dripping down my back.
It's time to jump in!

Theresa Rosario-Berzner
Long Beach, NY
Poet

~

I Love the Ocean

As a toddler, my parents would pack the car in the summer with food and family and we'd be off to Jones Beach. As a teen, it was Coney Island and Rockaway with friends. As I got more freedom, it was to the Jersey Shore, Myrtle and Virginia Beach and my favorite, Hilton Head, So. Carolina. As you notice, lakes and mountains don't do it for me. In my senior years, life gave me a great gift: my husband Harold. Plus, he loved to fish and has done so since he was a young boy. Every summer weekend we fish. Nothing like fresh-caught fish for dinner. Our first wedding anniversary, we celebrated with Sandy and five feet of water in our home. After repairs and recovery, life went back to normal. Looking over the past few years I realize: "I AM LIVING THE DREAM" IN LONG BEACH.

Carole A. Michelman
Long Beach, NY

Humility-Birthed

They lived in sandcastles—claimed purchased dominion
roughly fingering her shore—as the sea watched with
rolling patience——rippled, crashed into jetties, rose and
receded
existing as background for their lives and play or so they thought-
—thought with grandiose underestimation—until

One October day a single raindrop fell and the barrel overflowed
—a whisper wafted on the wind and insult whirled to rage
irrepressible—
All it took for her was a shrug of magnificent
shoulders to tumble-toss their toys—

Ah, their toys, homes, cars, boats, belongings, all their
trappings large and small floating up and away—
as she raised sandy mountains to cover their streets and vanished
vanquished homes as they stared in stunned stupefaction—

Pushed away, they grieved their losses, and in unshakable love
returned to rebuild, humbled in reflective irrevocable respect
for her gracious permission to survive along the rise and fall
of salted sacred tides.

Finally, the Sea satisfied, stretched, relaxed, lovely and loving
once again—and once again they lived in beloved sandcastles
Sunshine sparkled on wave tips-repeating and receding
into an unpredictable unknowable horizon.

Pearl Ketover Prilik
Lido Beach, NY
Poet

Glowing, Glowing...Gone

Back in my high school days I developed an affinity for astronomy and anything related to space. So much so that I went and bought a telescope, which I often took to the beach where I could enjoy an unobstructed view of the sky.

It was a warm summer evening. The sun was setting. Red streaks permeated the sky.

I planned to view Mars and Saturn with its rings. Having planted the legs of the tripod in the sand, I looked up and then it happened. Slowly and silently moving west to east over the ocean were three objects in triangular formation. Two above and one below. These objects appeared to be illuminated spheres, each resembling a full moon. There was no obvious means of propulsion.

I observed this event for maybe a minute. Then, to get a better view, I took my eyes off the sky so I could place a lens on the telescope. When I looked up again, the objects were gone. While looking away, they somehow disappeared. Did they speed off? I will never know.

Living not far from New York City and its many airports, I had witnessed many aircraft. I can tell you these objects were not airplanes, nor helicopters nor balloons. Where did they come from and what were they doing?

This was my first and only encounter with UFOs. The experience left me with more questions than answers.

Donald Barry Leider
Long Beach, NY

Anything goes when you are at the beach.

Sand between my toes
Anything goes when you're at the beach
The rough grains of sand underneath my feet
The smell of seaweed, the smell of the ocean,
the smell of suntan lotion

Who will I meet playing in the sand?
The sand is burning my feet
I ran into the water
what a treat

The water is flowing between my toes
Anything goes when you're at the beach.

Lisa Dawn Romano
Atlantic Beach, NY
Photographer

Beached Wail

cento

How sweet, despite the ocean's salt
an unexpected storm started up.
Breaking ground for a new day
Sudden crisp September air
brings hurricane season,

Mayhem and chaos
Death and desperation
Watching the waves come onto the shore,
Finally, the Sea satisfied, stretched,
relaxed, lovely and loving.

Red streaks permeated the sky.
The water is flowing between my toes.

Peter V. Dugan
Long Beach, NY
Nassau County Poet Laureate Emeritus 2017-2019

Point Lookout – Lookout

Long, long ago my mother, father and young brother would routinely take long trips out east from our apartment in a Brooklyn two-family to the *wilds* of a place called Point Lookout. During the summer, the beach was (I realized as an adult) restricted to residents only. My brother and I were instructed to keep very still as my father spoke. My father, brave and completely out-of-character as a truth-stretcher, would thrillingly and quite mysteriously fabricate tales of relatives and borrowed cars to the man in the booth, convincing him that we actually did live here—gaining us entry time and time again. Mistruths only along the strictest geographic demographic lines, because flinging open those car doors, running across the sand to the sparkling sea—marsh grasses blowing on both sides of us—we were, indeed, home.

Pearl Ketover Prilik
Lido Beach, NY
Poet

It's a 'Shore' Thing
The 'Shore' Story project

November 9th, 2022

"THE FIRST TIME I ..."

The First Time I Read at an Open Mic

A chick just knows when its time
From the darkness of her shell
To tap, tap, crack
And let the light in
5 spotlights on a track to be exact.
Looking out to her flock
She will just know what to do
They say chicks can hear each other as embryos
So nice to meet again,
my Long Beach Library friend.

Nina Goldenberg-
Long Beach, NY
Poet and Educator

The First Time

The first time I saw my son Peter's face I was filled with joy. It was a scary birth for both of us and when the nurse brought him close to my face, I knew this was a special baby. My mother was also in the hospital at the time. She had had a stroke. The doctors had said for us to keep her talking.

So, I asked a nurse to bring a note to my mother. The note said: It's a boy! Name him!

The following evening, the nurses came to my room. Told me to be quiet and get in the wheelchair. I did what they said. We arrived at the nursery and there was my mother, in her wheelchair. She said, "Name him Peter, we need a rock."

And Peter has been that rock. He is a corpsman in the Navy and a police officer for the City of Long Beach. He is my rock.

Kathy Ryan
Long Beach, NY
Poet

It was March 31, 1956, I was eight years old.
I was on the Belt Parkway when I saw NY for the first
time, the beauty of the oceans and the parks.

Nuala Moquin
Long Beach, NY
Improv Actress

14

The First Time

The first time
I held you close that night
tropical perfume of frangipani
filled the air—I held you close
your skin on my damp breast—
just the two of us alone in a dark
room—jalousied windows open
to night songs, I was young—
you were far younger—my
magically newly born son—
"Well, here we go kiddo," I
whispered in the night and you turned
face to my breast, kneaded my still
hot flesh with a dimpled fist, latched
hard and suckled love insatiable,
irrevocably, forever sealed in
the first time

Pearl Ketover Prilik
Lido Beach, NY
Poet

The First Time

The first time I came to this area I was about twenty. I remember hitting up Chauncy's on the beach. We'd drive here from Cypress Hills because it was the only place left you could go that let you drink on the sand. We'd strip to our undies and jump off the jetties, living free on a hot summer night. That was before you'd get a summons if you dipped after the lifeguards left. At that time, my regular spot was Rockaway at Beach 116, and my transportation was the A train. It is not surprising that I made my way here to Long Beach. Once I could drive, you'd find me at Channel 80 or Patty McGee's. I've been living here for over thirty-five years now. Thirty-five years of jumping waves, riding my bike on the boardwalk and sitting in my Tommy Bahama backpack beach chair, drinking peach wine out of plastic cups, watching the fireworks from the beach. I don't miss the nor'easters or Irene or Sandy. I do miss the pancake house, and the arcade and more recently I miss the smorgasbord. But I am always glad to be home, here in Long Beach.

Paula Curci
Long Beach, NY
Performance Poet

It Took a Mouse

There is no way I would ever compare myself to Walt Disney. That being said, there is one experience we both share.

Walt Disney began his career by drawing sketches of the mice he observed running around his office. The rest is history.

One morning, while standing in my kitchen, I noticed an object dart across the floor. It was a mouse. I immediately ran to the hardware store and purchased a zillion sticky glue traps, which I strategically placed around the kitchen. I then waited.

Sure enough, the following morning, under the refrigerator was a mouse stuck to one of those awful traps. The mouse died. It bothered me that I caused an innocent creature to suffer. I then wrote a story expressing my remorse.

Having shown the story to my coworkers, I received positive feedback. This emboldened me to write other stories, some were later published.

I was never an English major nor have I ever attended a creative writing class. I never intended to be a writer.

It took a mouse to unlock something that was hidden deep inside me.

Donald Barry Leider
Long Beach, NY
Prose Writer
(Adapted from a
previous story)

Resurgence

I usually start with my own pencils and paper, I'm usually able.
But these are the first that someone else gave me, now on my
table.

On a night I felt like I was draining away, you reinforced more of
me back in.

From this I've learned that when I can give, to make that giving a
given.

And if I feel like I can't give anymore, I'll choose to rest, but I'll
never give in.

I'll recharge, I'll re-appear, I'll return, but only after I've landed.
So, take what you're given today, and don't take those gifts for
granted.

Never wait for pencils and paper to be handed.

But uplift others who need support, do that when you're able.
Someone you meet someday may really need that,
Someone to place a pencil and paper on their table.

Evan Leider
Long Beach, NY
Poet

The First Time

The first time ever I read a poem,

It was to a group of poets and musicians in the Staten Island Underground.

The Cafe Verboten was a cool beatnik scene.

The poem was an ode to an ex, entitled "F. U. Bob."

Little did he know,

I was damning him to hell in a coffee haus basement.

It was dark and smarmy, smoky and damp, (like him).

I had to get that man out of my system

And I did!

Theresa Rosario-Berzner
Long Beach, NY
Poet

It's a 'Shore' Thing

The 'Shore' Story project

December 14th

A HOLIDAY MEMORY

My Wallet Was Found!

It was 12:45 pm. I looked in my pocketbook, my wallet was gone! I had a doctor's appointment for an MRI in Massapequa, with twenty-five minutes to get there. No driver's license, five credit cards were in there plus a hundred dollar and a twenty-dollar bill. I immediately called the doctor's office, and they said they had my license on file. I went. I had waited four weeks for this appointment. Two hours later, I canceled the credit cards, ordered a new license online. At about 7:30 pm my doorbell rang, there was "LARRY THE HUMAN." He found my wallet in the parking lot across the street from the library. He said he reached out on Instagram and wrote me a message. I never thought to look. In the message it said if he didn't hear from me, he would come to my home. What a human! All the credit cards were there and the hundred dollar and the twenty-dollar bills.

PS: I remembered that I was rushing to get to Mahjongg at the library at 11:00 am that Wednesday and noticed as I was crossing the street that my pocketbook was unzipped.

Terri Midoneck
Long Beach, NY
Retired Reading Teacher

HOLIDAYS

Holidays have stayed
the same
Joyful special events
But the families have changed
In my older age
Branches breaking off
Grandchildren
Have grown and gone
To college overseas and
beyond To different homes
With their new families
It's essential to have a spare
At holiday time
And throughout
the year?

Eleanor T. Sobel
Long Beach, NY
Poet

A Holiday Memory

Snow flurries gently descend
From a December's evening sky
And seemingly without end
As the scent of winter
Mixes with Long Beach's
Salty air
And holiday lights glow
In the windows everywhere
As I rush home
Down Florida Street
In anticipation
Of lighting candles
Eating latkes

Sharon Denson

Long Beach, NY
Prose and Poetry Writer

Micro Memory Poem

Holidays, Holy Days
Holidays, Holy Days
Kneel and praise
Proclaim your faith in family
A little baby in a manger
A Mother Mary, Father Joe
The Creator of the Universe, we all sing to you in awe.
A Christmas song, a Spiritual Hymn
A soulful, joyful noise!
The Spirit of the season is abounding,
Sounding out loud and clear!

Theresa Rosario-Berzner
Long Beach, NY
Poet

Snowflakes swirling now
Ice forming crystal chaos
Sisters north wind flow

Daryel Groom
Long Beach, NY
Teacher and Poet

Forever Silvered

Chanukah as a little girl in my grandparents' forest green velvet carpeted living room — My dapper mustachioed grandfather standing and with great ceremony pulling from deep in his pants pocket a real silver dollar — turning it between index finger and thumb so it caught the lamplight as he pressed it into my hand. I held the weight of it in my palm, ran my fingers across the grooves and listened as my Papa told me that the coins were special — this became our Chanukah present and tradition each year — saved, cherished and shimmering — and years later when the time came to surrender silver coins — they stayed safe as the silver memories they were holding; the light of flickering candles in the menorah, the story of Chanukah and the magic of forever love.

Pearl Ketover Prilik
Lido Beach, NY
Poet

Special Program:

Winter Solstice

with Poetry and Hot Chocolate
Magnolia Pier
December 21, 2022

Winter Solstice

Is almost here
cold winter skies
makes it perfectly clear

Beneath the ocean
blue sun disappears
Astounding sun's rays
set ablaze clouds
in golden hues

Full moon rising
glows in the east
stars appear
Hanukkah and Christmas lights
bring cheer
celebrating wintertime so very near!

Patricia Brown
Five Towns, NY
Poet

It's a 'Shore' Thing

The 'Shore' Story project

JANUARY 11, 2023

A TIME IN THE LAST YEAR (2022) WHEN YOU FOUND YOURSELF AMAZED ASTONISHED, ASTOUNDED, OR SURPRISED

California

Big Bear
I met her there
She was in the snow.
San Clemente
By the sea
Her hair golden brown.
Arcata
I like her,
Her redwoods running free

Patrick Edward Tarpey
Captain Zebulon's Ketcham House and Garden
A 240-year-old house
Amityville, NY
Author

A New Year To Do

A New Year to do, a resolution or two
The Planet's Revolutions and The People's too.
The People's evolutions, a chance to renew.
A fresh start, an opportunity to begin anew.
Beginnings are hewn, The seeds that I've sown,
My future's unknown!
A New Year, to do ... Woo Hoo!

Theresa Rosario-Berzner
Long Beach, NY Poet

This Past Year (Looking Back)

This past year I saw my boy become a man. The size of his hands, the breadth of his chest. Broad shoulders, not yet weighted down by responsibilities but starting to bear some burdens—the beginnings of adulthood. The conscious awakening into understanding, what it is that grownups do…and why, and how to do them. The realization of daily life and how to get shit done. It's go time now. No more fooling around (well, maybe some). We can still be adults and continue to have fun! Sorting through his childhood toys, respecting his process. Making progress! Learning from excess and learning to be generous and give some things away. Learning about self. He had become a caring man. He understands the feelings of others. He's become considerate, learning to forgive others, their flaws, and how to accept his own. His strengths are emerging, through growth he is purging his childish ways. We talk about life and we cherish these days and memories!

Theresa Rosario-Berzner
Long Beach, NY
Poet

Astonished – Astounded-Shocked-Surprised

November 14th… not a particularly notable day — My husband was catching up on the sleep that had eluded him the night before – – At one point he seemed and was a bit feverish. Nothing earth-shattering at 101 — He slept. An hour or two later: fever down. He slept. About 6:30, he rose, felt rested and hungry with a fever below normal — We ordered a turkey sandwich and some split-pea soup, and when it arrived sat in the living room watching TV and eating. "Is it very cold in here?" he asked. Suddenly he was cold — teeth rattling-in-a-death-rigor-grimace-I-had- never seen-anything- like-this-cold. I tried to give him a cup of hot water — his hands shook too badly to even hold the cup — He thought he'd get back to bed and under the covers — I had other ideas — by the time he was in bed 9-11 had responded — a fleet of boots clomped into our bedroom — Lights and sirens to the hospital — Stabilized on fluids and antibiotics. We waited for seven hours, chatting and trying to keep warm in an ironically freezing ER. Our cardiologist found us a waiting area staffed with nurses and a doc where we could continue our wait for a room. Husband feeling fine as the sole occupant of this warm and staffed holding area — Doc was pleased — We were pleased — Doc left — Two minutes later — Husband was cold. That kind of cold. Again. This time he suddenly sat up and I saw death in his face staring back at me through his eyes. Rapid Recovery team called — IV's, blood spurting through my fingers as they pushed all sorts of cardiac drugs into his veins — A forced oxygen mask — Controlled chaos.

And then he stabilized. Sepsis cascading into a cardiac event is astonishing, astounding, and beyond. The line and speed of travel between here and there is shockingly fast and slim. Astonishing? Amazing? Shocking? Yes, the trauma certainly was and yet for all the horror of looking death in the face — what is truly astonishing, amazing and filled with boundless wonder is the resurrection of life! The couch is comfortable again — It took a few months to regain an appetite for deli fare — but once again the turkey on rye is good, the mustard nice and spicy. Life returned, renewed, cherished and savored.

<u>Pearl Ketover Prilik</u>
Lido Beach, NY
Poet

It's a 'Shore' Thing

The 'Shore' Story project

February 8th, 2023
A recollection of ...
SOMETHING THAT HAPPENED IN
FEBRUARY

The shortest month of the year.

Here are some dates
that might spark a memory:
African American History Month
Purpose Day February 5
Groundhog Day February 2
Presidents Day February 20
Saint Valentine's Day February 14
Mardi Gras February 16
Leap year February 2016 and 2020
Super Bowl Sunday February 12

February Musings

February is warm
This year, pansies peeking up
 I fear climate change is here.
And another birthday looms.
Three quarter century can bring some gloom
dissolved by loving family and friends
whom attend my life's highs (I hide my lows)
and Valentine's Day always glows,
a day after my birthday.
I greet it with laughter.
The rest of February
leans toward Spring,
for cold has never been my thing .
My Bones grin when my coat is thin,.
Light of heart
I spring- spin,
despite my weight of years,
I greet longer days,
with cheer,
 and hope I'll still be here

Francine Friday Rosen
Lido Beach, NY
Retired teacher, artist, lover of gardens

I remember the smell of coffee brewing
and the sound of my mother's sweet
voice as she sang and prepared breakfast
for my Dad and our family.

<u>Rey Leleniewski</u>
Long Beach, NY
Originally from Arizona
Retired
Improv Actor

Goodbye February

We dwell now in the coldness of winter.
I shiver looking out my window
In the early morning
I see the bleakness of nature
Where only the pine green and sky blue are of color
People whisk by, bundled in down
Some with children off to school or work
My mind drifts to thoughts of division, tribalism and
hate from media and the people of the earth
With the denial of climate change
We await the wrath of nature
Stop now, change my negative mind
I need a moment to refresh
I close my eyes and create an imaginary
vision of the rebirth of spring
The breeze is balmy and full
With the scent of early cut grass
The peeking up of the crocus and tulip
I see the swaying of young chartreuse weeping willow
And the bright yellow of forsythia
I listen to the song of cardinal, robin, blue jay and more
The run and jump of squirrels along the fences line
The gentle billowing of clouds above
I slowly open my eyes and come back to the present
I am calm now, as I quietly sit in solitude
Waiting for my love to awaken
Ah, to experience the new day
together

Wayne Marcus
Lido Beach, NY
Creative Poet

Unpretty Valentines

Some girls, most girls, were far better at cutting folded paper to open into filigreed Valentine's Day hearts — I didn't get the memo and with tongue tensely sticking out of my mouth I worked, cut, and opened to a paper cut neatly into two pieces pocked-marked with holes — Valentines were not my thing — but love was — I still admire the girls who deftly turned their scissors and white paper — marveled at the magic of their pretty paper hearts pasted neatly onto crimson construction paper — l never got the hang of precise and pretty love — as I scrambled to paste my fragments of paper in an after the fact Valentine my heart beat fast with thoughts of love outside the paste.

Pearl Ketover Prilik
Lido Beach, NY
Poet

Well, I can remember today that, in fact, I remember nothing — nothing from before. Memories live forever, even the ones we're making in the present and presently I'm writing this. It's about a first-time stage for a seven-year aspiration. The willingness to push oneself to exist outside of their boundaries, on the fuel of one' s passion and the need to express that I too can leave a mark on this world, a memory. "And so, what if I don't?" My memory will be the courage and perfectionism. My memory will be the people and the support. My memory will be my fear of heights off a two-foot stage. My memory will be.

Nicholas Accovelli
East Northport, NY
World Language Educator/Poet.

Winter Nights

On cold winter nights, we would bundle up warm in our bathrobes and slippers, make pillow forts out of couch cushions and pop Jiffy Pop popcorn on top of the stove. Heating up the foil pan over the gas burner, we watched the bonnet of aluminum bloom into a big shiny silver balloon! We squealed with delight, oohed and ahhed, listening to the pops. Shaking it hard back and forth. We tried to make sure we popped every kernel. Once it was done, the steam was released with a pop and we opened our treat, poured it into a bowl to eat while we watched old black-and-white monster movies with our pop. Cozy with blankets, TV movies and sometimes tomato soup and grilled cheese sandwiches. Those were the days!

Theresa Rosario-Berzner
Long Beach,
NY Poet

Polar Bear Plunge
for the Make-A-Wish,
which involved my granddaughter,
Marsha,
who raises money for other children's wishes.

Marie Quigly
Long Beach, NY
Improv Actress, Comic

37

It's a 'Shore' Thing

The 'Shore' Story project

March 8th, 2023

A RECOLLECTION OF SOMETHING THAT HAPPENED IN YOUR CHILDHOOD

Waiting To Be Beaten

Tormented by the schoolyard bullies, before "bullying" existed as it does today, I was often left to battle. I never sought fisticuffs, however when spring smacked the air, I became a reluctant defender of my pudgy body. The insults and threats I could not ignore…I realized that I would have to engage in an activity that always made me hideous. In the center of the circle, I am waiting to be beaten.

Ralph Hooten
Lynbrook, NY
Laborer

Childhood Memories

My mother, my father
My brother and me were a close knit family
As the oldest child
I had to be perfect
In everything I did My father expected it
and I wanted to make him proud
He was an immigrant
from Eastern Europe

Alice Laby
Long Beach, NY
Poet and Writer

Childhood Flashback

Jacks and Hopscotch,
Sidewalk Chalk,
I never balked
at hot Brooklyn
Summers,
Mom's triple cones,
envious moans,
Bungalow in Rockaway
The Beach,
Hurray.
Winter Snow
Dry mittens
Thrown Stone
Like from
Apartment
windows,
Delicious Smell
of cooking
Always looking
To see what
Was in Mom's
Pot, Usually
A lot,
of loving smells,
I love to dwell
In
those
Days.

Francine Friday Rosen
Lido Beach, NY
Retired teacher. poet, artist, garden lover

A Divine Mystery

The summer my brother was preparing to move to heaven
an odd Hosta plant pushed through the soil
that housed a red Japanese maple.
I visited it daily, knowing it
was delivering a message.
It grew more
beautiful
until its bud became a flower,
more exotic than any orchid I had ever seen,
a perfect message, a perfect representation
of the love my brother
and I shared.
The Hosta has become my blessed connection to him.
No matter how distant he may be,
he is here.

Doreen Dd. Spungin
North Woodmere, NY
Poet

41

So empty and bare
sits my little dog's chair.
So fluffy and white,
I would hold him so close and tight.

Brielle Hills
Long Beach, NY
Sgt. US ARMY
Mother of a five-year-old boy
Poet

The kitchen floor
The slap of the plastic rope
My mom's patience
teaching me to jump rope
I COULD NOT DO IT!
'till I could
Now I live with her again.
She is still
patient,
Still teaching me

Nina Malkin
Oceanside, NY
Earthling

A Little Help From My Friend

When I was a young child, I was terrified of doctors.
Mostly, I was terrified of getting a shot.

When my father drove down a certain street.
I knew we were heading for the doctor.

 I would let out a scream and begin to
cry. On one occasion, I locked myself in
the car in front of the doctor's office.

After some tense negotiations I emerged.
My parents were beside themselves.

This all changed when I became friends
with some kid who lived in our building.
There was a brother and sister whose father was a doctor.
When I asked my mother if I could see him,
without hesitation she answered yes.
He was a very nice man who put me at ease.
I dared not utter a peep.

From that moment on I forever left my fears behind.

Donald Barry Leider
Long Beach, NY
Prose Writer

I must have been about ten years old.
My dad had gotten me 2 pairs of
boxing gloves for my birthday.
My friend Bobby and I wanted to try
them, but my mother didn't want me to
break any of the furniture.
So we went down into the basement, where
we couldn't break anything.
We exchanged a few jabs and then
Bobby threw a hard one at me.
As I ducked, I hit the corner of an old black-and-white TV set.
As I reached to touch the spot on my head,
my childlike fingers didn't quite understand the
size of the indentation in my forehead.
I ran upstairs and out of the house crying:
"Mommy, I have a hole in my head!"

Phil Kennelty
Long Beach, NY
Songwriter

When I think of childhood,

the word that appears is innocence.

I say the word in my mind as I say "play"
the movie of my youth.

No hatred (at least I didn't know of any).

No war (although there's always war).

The sun always found me
(or did I find it)
and the seasons were kind
(just like my family).
Innocent of evil and sorrow,
I walked a positive road, trusting life,
gathering the strengths
I was going to need
once innocence waved
goodbye.

Doreen Dd. Spungin
No. Woodmere, NY
Music-loving poet

I am Brooklyn born and I'm here to blow my horn
My claim to fame is that I'm related to a famous name
His name is Harold you see and that makes me proud of me

Irwin Pfeffer
Garden City, NY

My brother makes an exciting entrance

I was three and a half the September my brother was born — we all rushed into the elevator with the milkman in the early dawn — the lift was going up and the milkman excitedly began jumping up and down willing the elevator to change course — my father had practiced the route to the nearby hospital during various times of the day — off we went — my brother coming fast — my mother's long legs up on the dashboard — me patting her head from the back seat as my father drove straight in the opposite direction and pulled into his mother's driveway! My father screeched out in reverse and put the pedal to metal. At this point police officers sussed out our erratic race down the silent streets of Eastern Parkway and thus the NYPD escorted us — we arrived at the hospital, my brother already peeking out into the world — or at least the car seat. A wheelchair appeared and nurses helped my mother in and wheeled her at a run through the hospital doors, down a long corridor and into a waiting elevator — she jauntily waved and surprisingly (to me) the stainless doors closed, leaving her on one side and me, hugely insulted and shocked, on the other. Off she went, leaving me standing there, obviously excluded. This was not going according to plan. In fact, from the time we got into the car, the events were completely different from my carefully anticipated expectations that had me in the room with my mother as my new brother arrived — and I would be one of the first to see and hold him. Instead, there, on that early September morning, I stood alone in between two marble cigarette-butt receptacles filled with sand as tall as I — excited and, yes, grandly flooded with insult at my exclusion. Yes, there I stood, as time stopped —— beginning my life marked, and divided forever, into the before and after I became a big sister.

Pearl Ketover Prilik
Lido Beach, NY

This Is For SURE

My first summer away was Wildwood, New Jersey, I was 7.
I thought
    I was in heaven. It was a shore thing.

Next summer we went to Long Beach on the ocean. I just turned 8.
I felt
    great. It was a shore thing.

When I was 14, I met the rest of my life at the youth center.
We were
    married and moved to Long Beach. It was a shore thing.

I went into business there. 64 years later,
it couldn't have been greater.
    It was a shore thing.

My 3 children have their own families.
    They were a shore thing.

One of my hobbies is fishing. You know that was a shore thing.
    (but not always)

After my wife died, I met a woman from Middle Village, Queens,
and she
    became a shore thing.

Now I enjoy coming to the Long Beach Library
every 2nd Wednesday of the month at 6pm
    because it's a shore thing.

Harold Michelman
Long Beach, NY
Businessman, Poet and Artist
Read at the open mic 3/8/23

Dad was king in my childhood universe.
He crowded his daily commands
for he felt he had paid his dues.

Mom waited on him
hand and foot, hand and foot
as if she was electronically set.

Dad did not give thanks for her service
and was rude, and was rude.

But in school I learned the fable well
of democracy and equality.

I knew I too wanted to sit
I wanted to sit at the head of the table.

I would be Athena
At the prow of the ship.
I would head the way.

And college was preparing me
to be my own person
to be a person

Then I met my one destined for me.
There was no doubt, I knew immediately.
There was an aura surrounding him to say:
He is the one; he is the one.

Despite that he is much older

And from the old country

And trampled on — destruction
and murder in the holocaust.

Surprisingly, he wanted me to do my thing.
He was devoted to me
And wanted to please me, please me
I wanted to give him everything
I was his wing person.
We had chemistry
It was not about female and male roles
It was about our love

Eleanor T Sobel
Long Beach, NY
Writer and Poet

Special Outreach
Nursing Home Visit
March 21, 2023

Spring into
The rest of your life
You don't get to live twice
Whatever it may be that brought you here
It's how the cards were dealt
Now that does not mean it was not felt
The shuffle
The play
The cruel game
The dismay
The losses...
When coming to a nursing home
At the bay
Where fish swim
And sun shines
Where flowers grow
And it's Spring time!
Sow…
Enjoy what you can
We don't come back
Frolic in your
Wheels of Glory.
You made it
This far.

Nina Goldenberg
Long Beach, NY
Poet and Educator

The Memoir Writers Group, April 11, 2023

Facilitated by Barbara Spinelli
Freeport Memorial Library Freeport, NY

AT THE SHORE

At the Shore

As I sit at the Point Lookout shore
toes embedded in the sand,
the sea reflecting its momentary
mood, I feel the immensity of the
universe — in the thrust of the idle
waves.
That sea touches all the continents,
even when it's called by different names.
I am but a mere grain of sand
but I am also a reflection of the divine,
part of the ebb and flow,
a part of the life force, yet to be defined.

Barbara Spinelli
West Hempstead, NY
Author and Facilitator of the Freeport Library Memoir Group

I am not sure if I am a fan of the shore.
Too much packing,
too much sand, too much sun,
The more I think of it,
I am sure now
I could do without the shore.

Seymour Leog
Woodmere, NY
Advertising Agency Art Director

<u>SHORE THING</u>

"I must go down to the sea again…" is one of my favorite poems, echoing treasured memories of childhood summers at Brooklyn's Brighton Beach; and then, much later, summer vacations in Brittany and Normandy and (more recently) summers on Long Island beaches. Sounds of waves crashing, the scent of salty sweat, and brine and suntan lotion; seeing swooping gulls and sand-strewn shells makes me feel somewhat sad that these moments are only short lived, ephemeral, waiting to be repeated; wishing that these moments were longer lasting. Surely those halcyon days are forever imprinted on my mind and soul; forever looking for shore scenes, perhaps even a metaphor for a life philosophy. And to end on a humorous note: "Don't call me Shirley," a line from a famous movie... Does Shirley (whoever she is) wait for me on the sandy shores?

<u>Mireille Taub</u>
Long Island Resident
Freeport Memorial Library
Memoir Group Member

On my annual vacation at Virginia Beach, every year for six days I watch from my bed as the golden hues of the rising sun peep out from the southeast horizon of the Atlantic Ocean. Slowly its silvery golden rays form a highway mirage from the sky along the way to shore. I go back every year to relive this utopia experience.

Maureen Nembhard
Freeport, NY
"Retired almost 10 years and loving every moment."

When I was a girl living in Queens, with no aspirations of ever owning a home in the South Shore, my parents would pack me and my sister into the car at the crack of dawn along with an umbrella, two beach chairs, four beach blankets, a full hamper of food, and a jug of iced tea for the trip to Jones Beach. We would sit midway on the Zachs Bay Beach, halfway between the bathroom and the shore. My excursion into the water often ended up with a lifeguard whistle informing my parents that I got lost looking for the campsite, without my glasses.

Judy Goldfien
Merrick, NY
"Happy Retiree"

I was a Levittown kid — my parents were pioneer owners in that great suburban experiment.

My entire world ended with the Freeport boundaries where Levittown bordered Hicksville, East Meadow and Plainview.

At the age of 13 my friend and I ventured out in his dad's car to the South Shore -a party fishing boat in Freeport.

The boat was going out for bluefish and we two immature anglers were fitted out with the appropriate rods, reels and bait.

Howie and I yanked up some powerful "blues!"

His dad picked us up at the pier, where we waited with our proud buckets of fish.

When we arrived back in "Levittown world," we suddenly realized that the exotic fish were left behind in the land of Freeport.

We were localized again.

Marc Josloff
Freeport, NY
"Artist at heart"

It was at the shore where I met a gal. We didn't date for months. We did however talk of dreams. Neither of us traveled. It wasn't in our parents' sights with limited means and no world outside our city streets or county blocks.

Our shared dreams, though, made us sure that we would.

Shared on the telephone with wires from the kitchen table to a favorite chair allowed us to understand. Her dreams were my dreams, my dreams were hers.

Our shared dreams were to visit the seashores of places with turquoise waters, palm trees. The two of us with tropical drinks in hand.

For us, our dreams have come true. Traveling to shores of the Caribbean, Hawaii, the west and Australia. Yet home and now our favorite, Jones Beach, is 17 miles from home.

Phil Jimenez
Freeport, NY
"Dreamer"

At the shore
The grass grew tall as the boat got closer
It was so deep
when we stepped in to retrieve the debris that was washed
by the waves
So much to recover
It looked really green, welcoming and soft
We adventured deeply in the sand
What a wonderful experience to clean the shores of LI
with friends on such a gorgeous day

<u>Aline Cassinera</u>
Freeport, NY
"Adventurous"

At the Shore after Hurricane Sandy

The Humvee made a wide turn off Riverside onto Olive. It rolled slowly down the block. My house is the second from the corner; it didn't take long before it reached my curb. I stood solid. Unable to move, I was fearful of the movie rolling in my head; the story about a South American child stolen by the military. Then flash – to the African militia who kidnap women. The sound of the truck was the same as the one on CNN. *Not here, get your mind straight. You are at the shore. This is Long Island. Long Beach*, I told myself. *They are here to help.* Still, I stood still. Didn't know if I should wave them down or run inside. Then, the truck stopped. A man wearing fatigues jumped out. All I heard was the thump, thump, thump, thump of his boots stomping on the ground and moving toward me. I saw nothing but hunter green canvas, tall and tied to calf-high boots. He walked onto my property and reached his hand out to me for a shake. I stepped back and he took his hand down. In what seemed like slow motion he said, "I'm your neighbor's brother. I'm here to check on his house. Are you okay? Do you need anything?" I took a deep breath; told him we were managing. My fear subsided, and I couldn't tell you if we had any other words. I think he told me there was food at the plaza, charging stations. I don't recall. To this day I don't know if he was NY National Guard, Air Guard, Naval Militia. I've never even talked to my neighbor about it. I don't even know if I told my husband. Honestly, this is the first time I haven't I welled up, thinking about Sandy.

Paula Curci
Long Beach, NY
Nassau County Poet Laureate 2022-2024

National Poetry Month

Poetry as Memoir*TM*
Presentation by Paula Curci

The Performance Poets Association
Tuesdays with Poetry April 25, 2023

Hosted By Lorraine LoFrese Conlin and
Doreen Dd. Spungin
Bellmore Memorial Library, Bellmore, NY

AT THE BEACH

Observation At Long Beach

full mouth down

then up and down again

she had a strange way

of eating an ice cream cone

he laughed throwing his arm

around her

in a separate universe

they thought they were

Cliff Bleidner
North Bellmore, NY
Poet and Founder of The Performance Poets Association

Hated the beach – the scent, the sweat, the sand, oily fingers trying, very unsuccessfully, to read a book.

Then I had a grandkid, then another and another and another, and suddenly I loved the beach, going there and hanging out with the grandkids, running into the water, playing Frisbee. Loved it. Fun.

Larry McCoy
Rockville Center
"Writer, sort of"

In the Dunes

Who goes to the beach in the dead of winter? Only people missing a few weeks or the most dedicated would venture out like that, and I wasn't sure which we were. Trundling out of our car, parked in Field 1 of Jones Beach, we faced the gusting, freezing wind, as we followed a path that cut through the dunes down to the sandy beach. Leaving the path, we climbed onto the dune with its' tufts of goldenrod and knotwood, where other people stood, cameras out. Ours came out too. There it was. The owl.

Arnie Hollander
Long Island Resident
Poet
Board member of the Nassau County Poet Laureate Society

It wasn't love
But it felt like it
At 15 you fall in love in a heartbeat

Your whole life is before you
So many years
So many first loves yet to come

And so, it was for me that day at the beach
The sun, the sand, plus Salvatore
We talked, we kissed and we fell in love

Just like summer, that ends too soon
Our romance ended as quickly as it began
A short pause until it begins again

Patricia (Rispoli) Edick
"A Long Island Native of Italian descent.
Born in Brooklyn. Childhood in Queens…
Widow, mother, grandmother"
Children's book, short story writer and poet.

Ocean

A cool breeze,
the sun shines on the wispy waves
The warm sand beneath my feet
makes me forget my worries
Calmness overcomes my fears
bringing me closer to nature
Whispering sounds of seagulls
fly over head
My mind is clear
Nothing will clog my thoughts
Splashing children & adults
Ride the waves
I'm in the present
The ocean is my savior.

Sheila Hoffenberg
East Meadow, NY
Poet

Poetry as Memoir – Water, Water Everywhere…

What to write? What to say?
The beach is calling me today:
too busy, though, to walk on down.
Too much to do, my time is drowned!
I gardened in my yard the other day,
I planted seeds, basil, thyme and bulbs.
Irises, daffodils, tiger lilies and such…
I watered and watered and watered so much
I went to yoga to work up a sweat.
I had so much to do, I hadn't even
had a chance to get
to the BEACH YET!

Theresa Rosario-Berzner
Long Beach, NY
Poet

Ocean – Sea Shore – Beach

Ebbs of my mind
billows approaching
The waves offering
brine on my lips
sweet thoughts
take me away
as the current
steals the tide
In constant flux
I am reborn
I am
a mermaid

Rita Monte.
Baldwin Harbor, NY
Poet and Radio Announcer

First Kiss

We could hear the ocean's ancient rhythm. Waves like small angels floated to where we sat on the sand. We met at Spring Lake, NJ. He was stationed at Fort Monmouth. I was on vacation from nursing when he knocked at my door. The beach was a walk away. On stormy nights, lightning twisted in the sky for miles. But this night was salty with soft ocean winds, the moon and stars our only light. The sand curved under us; his arm curved around me. We turned to each other in harmony and our first kiss became the melody we would share for more than fifty years.

Paula Camacho
Farmingdale, NY
Poet
President of the Nassau County Poet Laureate Society

My Morning

I start my day with a sunrise view of the South Bay canal behind my home.

The tranquil water mirrors the houses on the opposite bulkheads.

Swans awaken and glide by, mallards dive deep in the salty water, then pop up

Again. Sea gulls pose on dock piles.

The tide comes in, sometimes with white caps, and tells me waves are crashing on Jones Beach.

Florence Gatto
Bellmore, NY
Teacher and Co-Director of the Long Island Writers Guild

At Jones Beach - A Haiku Sequence

Haiku

1. Summer sun smolders
   Sweat covers my body
   I rush to the ocean.

2. Standing on the ocean floor
   Water comforts me,
   I sway with the waves.

3. Between the sun
   and the water...
   I disappear.

Maria Monobianco
Farmingdale, NY
Poet

The echo...echo...echo...
In the tunnel (grubby and smelly, but no matter)
That led to the beach's magic, my blood
Pulsing to the waves' rhythm and
childhood's depthless joy...

Lisa James
Lifelong LI Resident
Poet

It's a 'Shore' Thing
The 'Shore' Story project

May 10 , 2023

AFTER THE RAIN

The Wake of COVID's Wrath

The clouds began their retreat.

The sun's rays reclaimed the sky.

In the wake of the storm were the broken businesses,

the vacant schools and the silent concert halls.

The weak left to deal with the long haul.

Our hearts go out to the victims and their families
who suffered so.

As survivors it is incumbent, we declare:

We will persevere.

Donald Barry Leider
Long Beach, NY
Prose Writer

After the Rain — My Light

Joints aching no longer fill me with dread; as I watch my youngsters amuse themselves in the water of life, I realize the joys filling my brain. Like a train, one cart connects to another, and suddenly, my mind floods, reflecting the streams of liquid carrying past and into the drain presented in front of my house. "Anne!" I hear as tears roll down my cheeks, watching as the two creations of love giggle. "We are wed, Annie!" They smile and laugh, rain subsiding. No longer are they jumping and screaming — as I welcome them home, I allow for my hands to brush against their forehead, gasping at the icy skin. "Clothes off! Now!" I demand, lips curled into a grin, preparing blankets and hot chocolate. The heater grew tired as I laid towels upon its front remembering times I would play, too.

Sun doesn't always shine, but my children are my light.

Kayra Callum Omer
Long Beach, NY
I am 15 years-old

After the Rain — Olden Days

Refreshments in the mist, it makes me reminisce. Of the times I could play in the rain I saw today. As my bones creak, I dream. Moments of frozen memories cross my mind, lips curling carefully, remembering splashes across my knees, playing with children the same age as me. Calling to them through the water, my smile expands, realizing the friends sitting on the cement. Dozens of snails, beyond my sight; what brings them to my village?

I grin, bringing them a delight — lettuce.

As I clock back into my reality, I grasp onto my cane — wrinkles inhabit my face, my fears of aging becoming the truth of my appearance 52 years prior to this day. Forgetting all I am, I turn my head to the side — what I was doing, I do not know — and watch as snails bite on some lettuce behind the window. How odd, I wonder. Who thought of doing such a thing?

Kayra Callum Omer
Long Beach, NY
Proud transgender father of 2 loving cats!

After the Rain

After the rain, the clouds must make way.
The sky clears up and winds die down,
The garden is sated, the drops cling to green.
The blue returns in such a way,
reflections in puddles shine back from the ground.
The seedlings I sowed are peeking up now.
Small plantlings appear in neat little rows.
My sunflowers have started to show
They always grow and grow and grow!
From half an inch they have begun,
In the merry, merry month of May!
By the end of October, they will be so tall!
Two stories high almost to my second
story window. Fourteen feet in height!
After the rain, what a delight!

Theresa Rosario-Berzner
Long Beach, NY
Poet

After the rain...

I was fully dressed. Well, casually, being that it was my day off from my part-time job as an usher for the Showcase Cinemas. I can at least say that. Please pardon the run on sentence. I picked up my soggy black NIKE low-top blazers that'll no longer be mine soon enough. I dumped my shoes in the beige recyclable cotton bag and teleported outside of the house like a z-fighter from the Turtle school. I sliced through these 3-inch puddles from Alhambra Road, until I made it to the N35 bus stop at Grand Avenue heading south to Baldwin Harbor. But that's not where I am going. The bus arrived. I entered and showed my bus ticket from my phone to the driver. Ran to my seat. The bus drove on. A couple of stops later, I got out at the plaza by Sunrise Highway and dashed to the American Thrift shop to donate. So that someone else can take care of it better than I did.

Kris Janvier
A poet from Long Island
"I wander a lot."

After the rain stopped,
I woke from my scrumptious afternoon nap.
Feeling refreshed,
I walked outside, and smelled the fragrance from the flowers,
and admired the dew sparkling on the lawn.
I looked for a rainbow but saw none.
I walked barefoot across the lawn and enjoyed
the cool sensation upon my feet.
It's going to be a wonderful day.

The End.

Elaine Fenick
Free Spirit

After the rain subsided, I rubbed my eyes, pulled the covers off the bed, and walked over to the window. I pulled apart the curtains. "Rain! Rain! That's all it ever does around here, rain, rain, rain!" I looked down at my yard and noticed some of my outdoor furniture had blown over. " Oh well," I thought. "At least all this rain is good for the lawn." All of a sudden, as I glanced up at the dreary sky — a patch of blue emerged. "Looks like it might be a nice day after all."

The End

Patti Halloran
HOPEFUL

After the Rain — A Haiku

Rain, rain, rain more rain
A torrential persistent rain
The rainbow will soon arrive

Rainbow Rita

Years ago, my good friend Ben
nicknamed me "Rainbow Rita"

He nicknamed me Rainbow Rita
because he said
I have many colorful facets to my personality.

I was flattered to have been given
the name Rainbow Rita
— thank you Ben!

Rita Monte
Talk Show Host Profumi D' Italia
WHPC 90.3 FM
Nassau County, NY

After the Rain

I suppose it's the child within that feels that "after the rain" joy. Rain can be many things: The refresher on a too-hot summer afternoon, the spoiler of outdoor plans, the challenger to drivers. No matter which costume it wears, when the rain stops and the sun reappears my heart feels that lift of joy— the promise of relief, of play, of travel are returned. And what about the magic of petrichor, that wondrous fragrance that magics the air once the rain has stopped! Rain, its music as drops hit the roof, its delivery of nourishment for trees and flowers, its essence of life-giving liquid filling wells and reservoirs, is beloved by earth and all its inhabitants — certainly beloved by me — whether during its dance or once its music stops.

Doreen Dd. Spungin
North Woodmere, NY
Poet – PPA Co-Host Tuesday with Poetry

After the Rain
After the Rain
the early morning sun peers
from out of the clouds
came a mist lingered
in the air
the grass
the trees
all greens
glistened everywhere!

Patricia Brown
Five Towns, NY
Shore Poet

After the Rain

After the rain I would go outside to pick up the baby's highchair,
walker, playpen and some assorted toys. As a single, tired, working
mom the rain became my helper, my relief — it
cleared what I was too tired to clean — but the rain was also my
counselor, my friend. I could feel the sun breaking through, the air
was fresh. I could breathe and feel renewed to continue —
my soul recharged.

Leslie Weiss
Storyteller

~

After the Rain

Clean & Serene — after the rain
The sun splashes on the glistening terrain
Chirping birds once again fill the air
Grime and smog washed away everywhere
Dazzling sights abound for me and you
After the rain — when Hope Springs anew

Jim Coulter
Performance Poet
Long Beach, NY

After the Rain (Reign)

What is a rain?
Is it moist
droplets permeating
sidewalks
Or is it a
purple robed
politician
wanting
to "reign"
forever?

To the latter
I say never
No matter
how clever
No matter
how strong

It's for dewy drops
I long
and
they stop
and steam arises
I'll have made
no political
compromises

After the Reign

Francine Friday Rosen
Lido Beach, NY
Garden Lover

June 14, 2023

NCPLS Youth Awards Ceremony

Directions:
Write a short micro memory about
WINNING

Winning

What is life
If you haven't won
Something
What is life
If luck
doesn't bring
the ring
of a happy
day of
winning?

What is
winning?
Is it
Sinning?
Is it accumulating
bucks,
Is it
luck?
Is it having
what you
want or
wanting what
you have? Or
what you can
grab?
Is it the
highest score
or more?

You can't bid
for kids
or love
but if you
have them
you are above
winning
You're beyond

All competition
A complete
condition
beyond money
It's life's
honey
No sport or
test can
best these rides
even if you
dig ditches
hard, you're
winning cards
are family.
Love and
friends
with no
end
being the
best is
no test
and lotteries
are a
surprise

But not always
happiness
advised
So, I say with a
Sigh,
No need
To ask
why,
I
have
won
a
ton

<u>Francine Friday Rosen</u>
Lido Beach, NY
Winning as a prompt
for the NCPLS Youth Awards Ceremony
June 14
Retired Teacher

Winner, Winner Chicken Dinner!

Winning feels good when you cross that finish line.
All the work you put in is worth it!
Training hard to be the best, running faster than the rest!
Medals on your chest, trophies on your desk.
Sweat equity, putting in the time, memories sublime.
Showing the world what you can do!
Remembering the glory days of youth, running in track club.
Racing to do your best; running for love!
Love of the wind in my hair, love of my legs moving fast.
Love of the moment of running without a care!
I love the feeling of winning!
Running is freedom!
Wind in my hair!
Winning is just the icing on the cake!
Winning is running your own race!

<u>Theresa Rosario-Berzner</u>
Long Beach, NY
Poet

Winning Me

I have won myself over today and every day forward. I'm going steady with self-acceptance, like a staple breakfast of sunny side ups, toast and hot Costa Rican coffee. Like — Yeh!

Winning!   I am winning against my contrary self. Giving myself every chance at what I want to do — Yeh! I will persevere even if I'm a fussy dame with windblown hair. I'll be in the hall of fame of Perseverance!

I'm taking chances and so, I'll never stop growing — Yeh! Ms. Pan — that's what I am. I'm playing the winning game — the kid reaching for the golden ring on life's merry-go-round. It's a process thing, you know. Just doing that gets a star! It feels good creating — it's not about the applause. Ha, but I'm a star. Yeh! Yeh!

I will love myself as a daughter, choosing to live life as me unconditionally. I am helping others too — what good people do. It feels good. Yeh! If I am only for myself, what kind of person can I be? I'll be as happy and busy as a honeybee landing in a field of flowers. I'm spreading the pollen of love and self-acceptance around — a winning legacy. Yeh! Yeh! Yeh!

Eleanor T. Sobel
Long Beach, NY
Poet

June 21, 2023

Summer solstice
Meeting
Edwards Blvd Boardwalk
Long Beach, NY

SUMMER SOLSTICE

Summer Solstice Today

Longest period of daylight
Shortest night
Midsummer night's dream

Tomorrow a new day,
A ritual
New bride
New life

Tomorrow I will be a … Mrs.

Rita Monte
Baldwin Harbor, NY
Poet and Writer
Recollection of her Anniversary: June 21, 1975

Neither wind
nor clouds
can cool this
special summer
solstice celebration
of gathered poets

Patricia Brown
Five Towns, NY
Shore Poet

The Tides are Rising

The tides are rising
The planet warming
Orange haze chokes
in apocalyptic terror
A child turns from a
Mother – a mother
Mourns a bullet-
shredded body

The tides are rising
Carrying all — as
this mind scurries
seeking peaceful
pathways, stumbling
on new terrors

Until an errant agitated
glance out the window
finds glory focused —
the cacophony of chaos
calms in this young robin
on the wet green lawn
stretching to full height
and in spite or
because of it all
a smile lifts a clarion call

To hope
standing in perfect simplicity
rising always beyond all tides

Pearl Ketover Prilik
Lido Beach, NY
Poet

At Edwards and Shore

Stunning women
I share the day with four
We talk of weather, love and war
deeply sure, these poets on the shore

Here, we hear today ominous thought
but we forge on to enjoy the beauty the day has brought

Rain and riptides breeze on my face
solstice springs the clock and slows the days pace

Paula Curci
Riverside and Olive
A Shore Poet

The solstice is here
to light our unity.
May this togetherness
be as powerful and strong
as the shore behind us.
With the sun in front of us
we can and will shine.

I am "shore" of it!

<u>Nina Goldenberg</u>
Long Beach, NY
Poet and Educator

July 12, 2023

**Special Presentation
Ekphrastic Night
with Piano, Painting
and Poetry**

The Last Night of
Micro Memoir
Submissions.

With
Scott Ferrone, Artist and Pianist
Kathleen Regan, Artist
And

Stuart Friedman, Artist

Write a poem about endings
or this evening's
performances

Long Beach Library, NY

<u>Query</u>

Poets are artists
painting
pictures, and
creating images
with words.
Their language
draws the reader
into a vision,
a perception of reality
sometimes abstract
and
impressionistic.
Not a clear
clean-cut snapshot
sometimes only
an illustration
designed by
a cacophony
of sound
and
sense
The meaning
buried beneath
the words
and
within the mind
of the reader.
Begging the
question:
Can you dig it?

<u>Peter V. Dugan</u>
Long Beach, NY
Poet

Where are you?

Skies are still blue

Rain wets the trees
Seasons change – I can't stop time
But where are you?

I hear the music we used to play
Our Sacred Piano Moments
It comforts the aching for a while
But where are you?

Joy is a mighty power
Music is my joy
Memories keep the joy alive
That is where you are

Doreen Dd. Spungin
No. Woodmere
Poet/Dreamer

Inspired by Scott Ferrone's piano playing

Seas the Day

Rolling, churning, ebbing, flowing
My thoughts move from one memory to the next

Visions of crashing moments in life
Sounds twirling over and over
As my mind reaches back

Scents of summer
Strawberry, melon
Blending with
 the salty spray on my lips

Light dims but the crashing, rolling, thundering sounds
remain

Beach ghosts float past as the night envelopes the day

Is it time to...

Teri Scrocco
Growing Artist/Writer

Inspired by the evening's piano music,
with Scott Ferrone, and endings muses

A Breezy Friday Night

I paid $25.00 for a non-member ticket to visit FOTO GRAFISKA. Specifically at the desk, I walked quickly to the elevator away from the crowded lobby I pressed the up button and waited, and waited, and waited. 5 to 10 minutes have gone by. Already deprived. Not from waiting tho. But from my 5-hour morning shift, from the movies. Train trip to the city. Walking trip thru the city. Until I made it to 23 South Park Avenue. Finally, the door opened and a security guard was there with a trainee. I entered along with 2 family groups, and a group of friends. The guard pressed the "5" button. The door closed. Seconds later, we're up. The door opened. Here it was. the exhibition I wanted to see. The Hip Hop's 50th anniversary show. Pictures of B-boys and B-girls, street gangs, DJ's, graffiti artists, the trains, cars, ghetto, rappers' artifacts of albums, 8-track tapes, boom box, generations. Future Generations.

Kris Janvier
Nassau County Resident
"I love Art"
Inspired by the prompt:
A Special Presentation: Ekphrastic Night

Figure in the circle dominates, dictates, manipulates
Peacefully bends before the flood
The skin is bleached furthest from the surface blood
The ticks, bees, mosquitoes…
I am going to live in the dirt
Where nature sacrifices centuries for the positivity of all
who are free enough to observe it

Ralph Hooten
Lynbrook, NY
Shore Poet
Written after musing Kathleen Regans Art

WRITERS AMONG US

Writing is such a joy. To hear laughter, see smiles and
applause when reading published or unpublished work gets
noticed, you achieve satisfaction. As readers listen with
such interest it is such a great feeling. Knowledge is
powerful. To express what's on your mind and recreate it
on paper is not just a talent but a whirlwind of emotions
that generates subconscious thoughts. It lets you into a
world of make believe or true-to-life experiences.
Characters become alive and in poetry whether it rhymes or not
it creates a different meaning to the individual.

Sheila Hoffenberg
East Meadow, NY
Poet
Inspired by the prompt:
A Special Presentation: Ekphrastic Night

Artistic Movement

Music mused and moved
by hues
sharing news
at the shore

and he sees me awake in the sky
and she breathes a kindness with her eye
love, she does when he takes the time

images breathe
sound is key
fingers his roots
warrior, her pose

and they are all here
at the seascape
in an artistic circle
of harmony

<u>Paula Curci</u>
Olive Street Carriage House, LB NY
A Shore Poet

Inspired by the Ekphrastic Poetry Night

An Ending

Saying goodbye to a home and a neighborhood that's been mine for nearly two decades is daunting. I'll miss the brownstone stoop, the elaborate tin ceilings and millwork, the wild backyard, the cherry tree, the mission presented by the feral cats who wander through — the love and laughs shared here. I won't miss the ancient furnace that awakes like a coughing dragon. But it's done — doors locked, keys ceded, name scrawled again and again, incomprehensible check deposited. And I realize that this handsome house was never mine; I was just lucky enough to experience its contours for a while. Moreover, I realize there is no "mine." Now I am alive elsewhere. Resistance isn't futile, but it is foolish. Every ending is a beginning.

Nina Malkin
Oceanside, NY
Earthling

Inspired by the prompt: Ending

<u>Endings</u>

We have to make friends with endings,

if we want to move forward.

Nothing lasts forever, although we wish it would.

Accepting loss and grieving

with the grace of adulthood,

rather than the inconsolable grief of a child.

Endings are the moments between

loss and grief and hope.

One door closes,

another one opens, or so they

say… Completion of a cycle …

The end of the line…

the resolution of time.

<u>Theresa Rosario-Berzner</u>
Long Beach, NY
Poet

Inspired by the prompt: Endings

Addendum and Micro-Memoir Poem
By Peter V. Dugan

"It's a 'Shore' Thing"*TM* is nothing more than a celebration of humanity. We gather on the second Wednesday of the month to celebrate the spoken and written words of poets and prose writers. We celebrate the music and lyrics of musicians and we celebrate the wordless pictures of artists. We celebrate the communication of thoughts, experiences and emotions displayed in all their works. We celebrate without fear or censure, we celebrate without judgment and we celebrate each other as individuals. We celebrate our being who we are. We celebrate the twenty-first century by introducing *Contemporary Expressionism,* as illustrated in the honest and true stories and poems of this micro-memoir anthology. It inspired me to write the following Cento poem, trying to incorporate all of this book's contributors, using lines from poems in this book to celebrate what we do and will continue to do, here in Long Beach. This book is a testimony of "It's a 'Shore' Thing"*TM* as a home to *Contemporary Expressionism.*

Rhythm By The Sea
Cento

I feel the immensity of the universe,
forever looking for shore scenes.
The rising sun peeps out from the southeast horizon
too much sand, too much sun
the exotic fish were left behind,

 the debris that was washed by the waves
then up and down again
the beach – the scent, the sweat.
The sun, the sand,
nothing will clog my thoughts

as the current steals the tide.
This night was salty with soft ocean winds
waves were crashing on Jones Beach.
We faced the gusting, freezing wind
but water comforts me.

That led to the beach's magic
in the wake of the storm were the broken businesses.
Preparing blankets and hot chocolate,
moments of frozen memories cross my mind.
The sky clears up and winds die down,

I sliced through these 3-inch puddles.
 I walked barefoot across the lawn.
The rainbow will soon arrive.
At least all this rain is good,
from out of the clouds came a misty rain,

its music as drops hit the roof
I could feel the sun breaking through,
droplets permeating sidewalks
no need to ask why, this is
a Midsummer night's dream

standing in perfect simplicity
 but we forge on to enjoy.
Neither wind nor clouds can cool,
the solstice is here to light our unity.
I hear the music we used to play.

Beach ghosts float past as the night envelopes the day
Figures in the circle dominate,
and they are all here at the seascape
And I realize that it was never mine;
Completion of a cycle

Definitions

Contemporary Expressionism, termed by Paula Curci and Peter V. Dugan, is a modern poetry movement of the 21st century. After observing the phenomenal change that occurred in the post-Covid poetry scene, Paula and Peter noted that the long-form confessional narrative and short-form micro-memoir poetry were becoming popular.

21st Century *Contemporary Expressionism* is more than just the 20th century's definition, where the artist presents their emotional experience or memory through their work. *Contemporary Expressionism* in the modern poetry open mic scene is performed by the writer and is overt non-fiction. It results in an expressed communal and empathic appreciation for the writer-performers' poetic story. There is an exchange of mutual understanding between the poetry listener and the writer-performer.

Paula and Peter decided to focus on the micro-memoir genre as a way to entice open mic participants to express themselves and share personal disclosures to form affiliation and camaraderie at their open mic location. Hence, the micro-memoir project was born and *Contemporary Expressionism* organically developed.

What Is Poetry as Memoir?

"Poetry as memoir is a vehicle for expression, a way for us to tell our story. A micro-memoir poem is a brief snapshot of a recollection, using a single story from one's life, written in the first person." — Paula Curci

"What is a story poem? Here's my definition: A story poem combines highly compressed narrative, musing, and observation using poetic techniques such as alliteration, imagery, and metaphor. In the story poem, as in prose, the sentence rather than the line is the primary unit."
— Matilda Butler, *Story Poems as Memoir – Memoir Writing Blog.* With Kendra Bonnett. 7/19/09 https://womensmemoirs.com/memoir-writing prompts/story- poems-as-memoir

"… micro memoir—the hottest new category in publishing. Micro memoirs are very short standalone pieces, often exploring a moment in time, drawn from personal experience." ---Estelle Eramus -Blogger https://estelleserasmus.com/micro-memoir-what-you-need- to-know/

"A poet's autobiography is his poetry. Anything else is just a footnote."– Yevgeny Yentushenko, Poet

What is Poetic Folklore?

"Our micro-memoirs are folk memoirs, a form of poetic folklore. Even the act of writing them is a folk memory because they were shared in a common place, for a common goal, through a common process. They make us a community. " — Paula Curci

"What is the value of folk-poetry activity to members of the community? ... It is a means for members of the community to identify themselves with the joys and sorrows of their fellow inhabitants. In general, it usually brings people together. It fills a vacuum in people's lives. It is a shared activity." — Robin Gwyndaf,
"Poetry in Action: Verse and Narration in Everyday Communication, "Folklore.ee/folklore/vol/gwyndof.pdf (2006)

Folklore " ...it is actually one of the principal means by which an individual and a group discovers or establishes his or its identity. — Alan Dundes, American Folklorist, "Defining Identity Through Folklore," *Journal of Folklore Research* (1984)

10/12/2022 Micro Memoir Poem #1 L.B.P.L. Open Mic

T. Rosario-Berzner

Hosted by Paula Curci & Peter Dugan

The Beach - Wiggling my toes in the sand,
I spread out my blanket and smooth it out
with my hands.

Watching the waves come onto the shore....

Hearing the swoosh as they return to the sea,

Feeling the warmth of the sun, heating my skin.

The drops of perspiration run down the length
of my neck and chin, Dripping down my back. →

October 12, 2022, was the first gathering of "Poetry: It's A 'Shore' Thing!"[TM] Theresa Rosario-Berzner, a Shore Poet and our associate host, wrote this card as one of the first entries received.

Index

About us:

Paula Curci

Paula Curci is the 2022-2024 Nassau County, NY, Poet Laureate. She is a Poet Correspondent for *The Scene*. Paula is the producer of *Calliope's Corner: The Place Where Poets and Songwriters Meet*™ and *What's The Buzz*® on WRHU 88.7fm Radio Hofstra University and was honored as their Poet in Residence in 2022. She is the director of the Acoustic Poets Network ™ and hosts open mics at both the Hicksville and Long Beach, NY, Libraries. She co-founded the Long Beach Shore Poets and is the co-editor of the micro memoir project's "Poetry: It's a 'Shore' Thing! In an Unsure World". Paula is a Journal to the Self™ Journal Writing Instructor and facilitates poetry circles, free verse, introspective, and *Poetry as Memoir*™ writing workshops. She performs using the aesthetic she calls Posics™ and has released *Emissary*, *Bittersweet* and *Done That: Poetry and Posics*™ *The Audio Version*, under the Acoustic Poets Network™ brand. Paula has three chapbooks entitled *One Woman's Cathartic Release in Poetry*, *The Gift of Thanksgiving* and *Done That: Poetry and Posics*™ She is a judge for the 2024 Scholastic Art Awards and the Nassau County Poet Laureate Society's poetry contests. Paula has been honored by the March of Dimes, Nassau County School Counselor's Association, Artists in Partnership, the Northport Arts Council, Nassau County, NY and the City of Long Beach, NY. She has received a Gracie, several Press Club of Long Island awards and two New York State Council on the Arts grants for The Word-A Festival of the Spoken and Written Word: Celebrating All Voices, and for her upcoming book of portrait, I am poetry. Paula volunteers for CAPS Safe LI, the Nassau County Human Rights Commission's Youth Conference, the Long Beach Poetry Festival, Artist in Partnership and Nassau County Poet Laureate Society.

Peter V. Dugan

Peter V. Dugan is the 2017-2019 Poet Laureate of Nassau County NY, and the co-founder of the independent publisher Words With Wing Press, the publisher of "Poetry: It's a 'Shore' Thing! In an Unsure World." Peter is widely known for his work as editor and formatter for various Long Island anthology works including but not limited to: *Writing Outside the Lines* Wyld Syde Press 2012 *LI Sounds Poetry Anthology,* Wyld Syde Press 2023, 2015, and various other professional poets' projects. He is the host of It's Poetry Baby! at the Oceanside, NY, Public Library and the co-host of "Poetry: It's a 'Shore' Thing!"*ᵀᴹ* at the Long Beach Public Library. As curator of the online group, Long Island Poetry Listings, Peter posts upcoming events for anything poetry. As Laureate, Peter, in conjunction with the Suffolk County Poet Laureate, developed and implemented the co-county Poet Mentor-Youth Mentee Program. Peter is a 2016 2X Pushcart Poetry Nominee with nine books of poetry titled: *Medusa's Overbite,* Wysteria Ltd; lst edition, *The Prowess of Immodest Emptiness* published by Chatter House Press, *A Eulogy for Poetry:* Just Fiction Edition, *Something Wicked — Something American, Members Only, Oasis of Chaos, Tabula Rasa:, Vistas* and *Damned to Obscurity* on Words With Wings Press Peter is a member of the "Poetry: It's a 'Shore' Thing!"*ᵀᴹ* poetry festival committee at the Long Beach Public Library and was the co-assistant director of The Word - A Festival of the Spoken and Written Word: Celebrating All Voices. He is currently a facilitator for the Acoustic Poets Network™ Visitation Project and on the board of The Long Island Poetry & Literature Repository. Peter is also a judge for the Poetry Out Loud program, Nassau County

Dr. Pearl Ketover Prilik, DSW

Pearl Ketover Prilik is a poet, author and psychoanalyst. She is the concept creator of the micro-memoir's sub-title *In an Unsure World.* PKP is also a contributor of poetry and prose, and is the writer of the collection's foreword. She has held the title of assistant editor on various projects and most recently, as a member of the Shore Poets, she worked on the "Poetry: It's a 'Shore' Thing! In an Unsure World" micro-memoir anthology. Dr. Pearl has been the editor for the *Post Doc Psychoanalytical Society Newsletter* and other publications. As part of the Shore Poets planning committee for The Word-A Festival of the Spoken and Written Word: Celebrating All Voices she assisted with community engagement and facilitating interactive activities. As a public speaker PKP appeared on *Calliope's Corner: The Place Where Poets and Songwriters Meet* to share her poems and discuss her professional observations on how the Covid pandemic has effected society and her hopes for a brighter future. As a poet PKP has written three chapbooks of poetry: *Rachmones, from* Words with Wings Press, and *Gobsmacked,* and *Glimmers in the Stream,* both from Local Gems Press. Dr. Pearl has been published in a variety of anthologies including *Poetry Quarterly, Tucks, Scissors and Spackle, Pyrokinection, Red Wolf Journal, The Word of Myth, Post Card Shorts, Burningword Literary Journal, Bards Annuals,* and *the Haiku Journal.* Her work is also found in international poetry journals such as *Prompted, Really Love Your Book* and *Beyond the Dark Room.* As a psychoanalyst Dr. Pearl has written several self-help books: *Becoming an Adult Step Child: Adjusting to a New Marriage* and *Step Mothering: A Different Kind of Love* from Foreman Press and Berkley Publications and *The Art of Step Mothering from* WRS publications. Dr. Pearl is also a blogger; you can find her blog on http://drpkp.com (Imagine)

Theresa Rosario-Berzner

Theresa Rosario- Berzner is a Co-Host of the It's a 'Shore' Thing, Poetry Open Mic at the Long Beach Public Library. As a poet and multi-mixed media artist Theresa conducted workshops with the Shore Poets team to curate classic poems to combine them with original art works for both *The Ekphrastic Poetry Garden*, and *The Poet Tree* art installations for The Word-A Festival of the Spoken and Written Word: Celebrating All Voices. At the festival Theresa created poetry prompts and facilitated interactive poetry activities for children and adults: including *Pick a Poem- Take One Home,* which was flower boxes containing handcrafted flowers along with an attached poem, and the idea for 'I Am' face masks poetry template. Also Theresa was a member of the planning committee for the Long Beach Roxx Rock Festival and a production assistant for the show. As a guest co-host on *Calliope's Corner: The Place Where Poets and Songwriters Meet*, Theresa spearheaded the show topics on post Hurricane Sandy and how to deal with stress during Covid. She has appeared on several *Calliope's Corner* special broadcasts of *Poems from People Like You,* reading her original poems and those of contributors. Theresa was the Long Beach PTA's Chairperson for The Reflections Art Program. She curated and prepared student's art for National Competition and created student exhibitions. Theresa was a drawing and painting assistant art instructor at The People's Church Bible Arts Program and assisted with art displays and hosted exhibitions. Theresa's Paintings *Let the Children Come to Me* and *The Annunciation* won first and third prize respectively. Theresa's poetry and writings have been published in *Soul Fountain's: September 11, Commemorative Edition*, and *The Women's Anthology Edition*. She has had articles published in *Long Beach Style Arts and Entertainment Magazine.* Most recently Theresa's Haiku entitled *Tea with Honey* was published in *The Tea-Ku Book of Haikus About Tea* published by Local Gems Press.

Made in the USA
Middletown, DE
29 March 2024

51915806R00071